THE
MONARCH MIGRATION
A JOURNEY THROUGH THE MONARCH BUTTERFLY'S WINTER HOME

BY COURT WHELAN, PH.D.

First printed June 2019. Reprinted November 2021.

Copyright ©2021 Court Whelan

The right of Court Whelan to be identified as author of this work has been asserted in accordance with sections 77 & 78 of the Copyright, Designs and Patents Act 1988.

All rights reserved. No part of this book may be reprinted or reproduced or utilized in any form or by any electronic, mechanical, or other means, now known or hereafter invented, including photocopying and recording, or in any information storage or retrieval system, without permission in writing from the publishers.

Notices
Practitioners and researchers must always rely on their own experience and knowledge in evaluating and using any information, methods, compounds, or experiments described herein. In using such informationor methods they should be mindful of their own safety and the safety of others, including parties for whom they have a professional responsibility.
Product or corporate names may be trademarks or registered trademarks, and are used only for identification and expanation without intent to infringe.

Library of Congress Cataloging-in-Publiction Data
a catalog record for this book is available from the Library of Congress.

ISBN: 978-1-5136-4499-8

This book was conceived, designed and produced by:

Publisher: Natural Habitat Adventures
Creative Director & Author: Court Whelan
Photography: Court Whelan
Editor: Wendy Redal
Art Director: Mark Hickey

Printed and bound in Canada

THE
MONARCH MIGRATION
A JOURNEY THROUGH THE MONARCH BUTTERFLY'S WINTER HOME

BY COURT WHELAN, PH.D.

INTRODUCTION..5

BEHAVIORS & ADAPTATIONS........................29

ECOTOURISM & LOCAL INVOLVEMENT.......79

MONARCH CONSERVATION..........................113

FINAL WORDS..137

RESOURCES & REFERENCES.................156-157

Monarch butterflies represent
many things to many people. To some, they
are a symbol of rebirth and the afterlife, with
Mexican folklore and festivals revolving around
the timing of their annual migration. For others,
they represent change and metamorphosis, as
they are like all butterflies, going through a larval
and pupal stage en route to becoming a fully
fledged adult butterfly. To most, they are simply a
beautiful reminder of nature's delicacy. The regal
monarch butterfly is one of the most recognizable
butterflies due to its prevalence and cosmopolitan
nature, and it is also one of the most beloved
animals on Earth. Found in our backyards,
classrooms, science books, business logos,
sports team trademarks and more, monarchs
are ubiquitous. This book celebrates one of
their greatest achievements and still greatest
mysteries...their monumental annual migration and
overwintering event in the high mountains of the
Mexican Sierra.

Beginning each fall in the eastern U.S. and Canada,
hundreds of millions of monarchs migrate up to
3,000 miles to Central Mexico's remote mountains
in order to spend the winter. In a semi-hibernating
state, these millions will pass the time clinging
to fir boughs, needles and tree trunks, awaiting
springtime. What appears initially as a relatively
simple and straightforward migration becomes
infinitely complicated. It occurs in many intricate
and advanced ways.

The first amazing fact to recognize is that while
only a single generation makes the entire
southward journey to Mexico to overwinter
each year, there are in fact several subsequent
generations that make the return trip north to
repopulate the U.S. and Canada in spring and
summer. Thus, because there are generations
that live between the "migratory generation" that
goes to Mexico, neither teaching nor learning
takes place to show these butterflies how and
where to go. The great-grandchildren of the last

butterflies to migrate the year before repeat this migration the following year. This incredible ability to initiate migration and orient thousands of miles back to their ancestral home is attributed to a fascinating genetic code. Although headway is made each year in deciphering the complexities of this phenomenon, the monarch remains an enigmatic icon of the wonders of our planet. Through the pages of this book, I hope to give you a glimpse into this spectacle.

As with a great many animals on Earth today, there exists a very real threat to the monarch's survival as a species. Threats abound, ranging from pesticides used in agriculture to the ever-present issue of climate change. However, increasing knowledge and advocacy may collectively save the monarch and preserve this fascinating piece of natural history in our world. It is my genuine hope that this book will transform you into an influencer---a viewer with a voice for these incredible animals. Ecotourism is a powerful force for good in the world, and the monarch migration is a prime example. Each year, thousands of people witness this phenomenon, and their lives are forever changed because of it. If you can get yourself down to see it in person, I highly encourage you to do so. But for those who cannot, I hope the 15 years of photography I've collected here will nevertheless inspire you to admire the monarch as much as I do.

At first glimpse, the overwintering monarchs barely look like butterflies at all. They hang in clusters of thousands, weighing down branches and swaying gently in the breeze.

While the majority of monarchs remain relatively sedentary, roosting in the trees over the course of the winter, many will take flight on warmer days. Although they represent only a fraction of the total colony, it still amounts to hundreds of thousands in the air all at once.

The winter home of the monarch is nestled into the high pine and fir forests of the Sierra Madre, about 100 miles west of Mexico City. Here, extenstive stands of oyamel trees (*Abies religiosa*) help to provide an ideal microclimate and protect the colony from erratic winter storms.

Although rare, rain and snow during the monarchs' overwintering time can indeed occur. The integrity of the forest couldn't be more important during such events, as the trees act like a blanket, helping to insulate the butterflies from the adverse weather.

Although lightly populated
compared to more dense urban
centers, several small towns
exist within close proximity of
the monarch biosphere reserves.
The most famous is Angangueo,
a former mining town that now
embraces monarch ecotourism as
one of the primary income earners
for locals.

The location of the monarch overwintering grounds wasn't always known. Discovered in 1975, the butterfly groves were first revealed to the world in the August 1976 issue of *National Geographic*, bringing international attention to this fascinating phenomenon.

Although monarchs are in Mexico to "hibernate," the phenomenon is considered a quasi-hibernation compared to animals like black bears or ground squirrels that more fully hibernate. Despite being in a state of diapause, monarchs are actually quite active, as you'll see in the following photographs. Even for a semi-hibernating animal, they engage in a variety of activities that make them visually dynamic. From covering shady tree trunks to hanging freely in clusters at the tips of branches to basking in the sunlight with wings open wide, the monarchs' brilliance displays in many show-stopping ways. And despite their alluring appearance when layered upon vegetation, it is an otherworldly sight to watch the butterflies take flight. This single behavior can transpire in a number of ways, from single bursts of dozens taking flight to hundreds of thousands cascading into the air over just a few minutes. Once in the air, their flight can be further categorized. Monarchs often engage in a gliding flight in order to regulate their temperature, allowing the cool mountain air to pass over their wings, just like an air conditioner. This convection purposefully reduces body temperature. In rare instances you may also witness a uni directional flight, where an entire portion of the monarch colony may begin flying in a single direction in an attempt to relocate the colony to a shadier spot in the forest. In this case, the observer is treated to a river of butterflies, as they flood the air with orange and black brilliance. Thrusting human observers into sensory overload, perhaps the most interesting result of monarchs taking flight is the sound they make. When thousands take wing, as is common nearly daily during their overwintering period, the effect sounds much like the rustling of fall leaves. The combined resonance of hundreds of thousands of butterfly wings can stop you in your tracks...it's one of the most arresting and beautiful sounds I've ever heard.

As temperatures in the mountains warm from
an early morning low of 32° F to a typical
high in the 60°s (0° to 20° C), the monarchs
become increasingly active and take flight in
even greater numbers. By cooling themselves
through flight, they avoid the otherwise rapid
use of their stored energy in the form of fats
and lipids amassed during their southbound
journey from North America. Energy storage
built up during their fall journey is vital to
their survival, as only a small percentage
of monarchs are able to feed while in their
overwintering grounds. This is due simply to
minimal resources available in comparison to
the deluge of hundreds of millions of butterflies
congregating in a relatively small area. Not
only must their energy stores sustain them for
the four to five months while overwintering in
Mexico, but this same energy must also power
them on the last leg of their great migration--
their return north in the spring.

Using all available space in their prime habitat, monarchs cluster not just on the branches and needles of the fir trees, but also on the trunks. Oftentimes they become so dense that not a single bit of bark is visible.

A spectacular sight, monarchs become quite active on sunny, warm days. As sunlight begins to reach parts of the colony, monarchs exposed to increased temperatures will take flight in order to relocate to a more shady, protected area.

Prior to relocating, they must warm their bodies and flight muscles, and can often be seen basking on smaller shrubs throughout the colony. Once they are warm enough to fly, they'll take off to rejoin the millions still roosting in the trees.

Although the oyamel fir is their preferred roosting tree, they are commonly seen in pine trees also found in the area.

Using the cool mountain air to their advantage, monarchs will soar at mid day in order to cool off. If they become too warm, they will burn off fat and engery reserves that are critical to fueling their return journey north at the end of their overwintering period.

Surprisingly, monarchs rarely feed during their time in Mexico. They depend entirely upon the nectar they were able to fuel up on during their southward journey to last them through the winter. However, on warmer days common later in the season, monarchs can be seen "puddling" at small mountain springs, sipping on small amounts of water.

Despite their seemingly high level of activity, between flying, relocating to different parts of the colony or sipping water, the ideal pursuit for the monarchs is to remain relatively sedentary in shady, cool areas for the roughly five months they are in their winter home.

Monarchs will often exhibit the highest level of flight activity just as a cloud passes over on an otherwise warm and sunny day. Most researchers agree the butterfly is sensing this as the start of a cool period, whether it be just a long spell of cloudiness, or perhaps even dusk, ahead of a long cold night. In taking flight, they are relocating to a more protected part of the colony while they still have the chance.

Simply put, there just isn't enough nectar to go around in the monarch's winter home. Thus, while some monarchs can be seen feeding on nectar, it is a small fraction of the overall population.

Throughout the course of the winter, some butterflies will be knocked down from their roosting positions. This can be caused by wind, rain or even an unexpected nudge from a neighbor. Once on the ground, they must climb to a high point where sunlight can warm them before taking flight to again take a spot within the clusters high above the ground.

Once warm enough to fly, they will one by one take flight and rejoin the main colony clusters. In the meantime, they often look as though they are nature's ornaments on the rarest of Christmas trees.

Monarchs exhibit what's known as aposematic coloration. The opposite of 'cryptic' coloration, which aims to camouflage an animal in its surroundings, apoesmatic coloration functions to make the animal noticeably stand out and serve as a warning. Much like some frogs and snakes, where bright red or yellow coloration signals danger, the monarch uses its prominent black and orange coloration as a threat signal.

Monarchs are dangerous not in their bite or aggression, but because they are chemically defended. That is, they are toxic if eaten. Via the host plant leaves that monarch caterpillars eat (various milkweed species), they sequester a type of heart toxin known as cardiac glycoside. For a small mammal, reptile or bird predator, this can induce heart arrhythmia that can lead to vomiting and potentially even death.

Migrating monarchs are perhaps best known
for their gregarious behavior as they cling to
branches and tree trunks high in the forest.
They can also congretate in significant
numbers around water sources. While mountain
springs are common in the region, even the
small amount of water that accumulates from
morning dew is enough to satisfy their thirst, if
only for a short while.

Water is critical to monarchs, but too much can be a bad thing. Although monarch wings have a 'hydrophobic' covering, which repels water just like a rain jacket, too much water can render this coating ineffective, thus saturating their wings and hindering flight.

A shiny coating of monarch wing scales covers the top of the water, almost like a film, due to the hydrophobic nature of these scales. Monarchs often lose scales during the course of the season as they fly about, falling like glitter through the air, landing on the surface of plants and water puddles.

There is nothing quite like the first glimpse of the immense monarch colonies. As we round the corner of the trail, they come into view, and it's difficult to believe the orange and black masses before you are actually millions of individual butterflies.

Monarchs employ a fascinating navigation system, using the sun as a compass that allows them to orient on their way from Canada and the U.S. toward Mexico.

On cloudy days, they are able to use polarized light (which still passes through the clouds) as well as an internal magnetic compass to hone in on the highly magnetic Sierra Madre mountain range.

Although studied since the mid-1980s, the monarchs' use of an internal magnetic compass is still under investigation.

At the base of their wings, monarchs have been shown to possess magnetite, sequestered from their host plants during their caterpillar stage. However, exactly how they use this remains contested. The latest evidence at the time of this publication shows that they do indeed employ an internal magenetic compass, but only in concert with the perception of specific wavelengths of light. Some believe this may be yet another adaptation to be able to navigate on cloudy days.

With a time-compensated sun compass and magnetic compass being the first two navigation techniques employed by these butterflies, the third and final navigation tool has to do with smell.

Monarchs have a keen sense of smell via chemoreception, faciliated by their highly sensitive antennae. Most researchers agree that the leftover smell from previous generations of butterflies in Mexico provides the monarchs with detailed information on exactly where in the mountain range they should end up. While the sun and magnetic compass provide general bearings, an olfactory sense may lead a butterfly to the exact roosting spot where its great-grandparents overwintered the previous year.

Above is a close-up view of a male monarch's scent-producing androconial scales—the two small dark lobes present on the hindwing of the butterfly.

GUARDA
SILENCIO

The annual migration of the monarch

butterfly is a growing attraction. Located 100 miles west of Mexico City, the overwintering sites are drawing increasing numbers of day and weekend visitors to witness the colonies of millions of butterflies. Ecotourism surrounding this phenomenon has grown since the monarchs' winter home was discovered in 1975 by two Americans working with Dr. Fred Urquhart of Canada, one of the first biologists to focus on monarch butterflies.

The monarchs do not aggregate in just one colony, but rather in a dozen distinct sites throughout the transvolcanic range of the Sierra Madre. The butterflies reside in these sites over the course of the winter. With initial arrivals at the roosting sites in November, the colonies grow for about a month until they are at full winter capacity. Three of the larger colonies routinely exhibit more than 50 million individual monarchs each throughout the overwintering period. Once they arrive in the colonies, monarchs spend the remainder of the winter in reproductive diapause, a temporary halt in reproductive behavior triggered during the southward migration by shortening day lengths, greater temperature fluctuations, host plant senescence, and winter's lower sun angles.

At the end of their overwintering period, and as the spring equinox approaches in March, their reproductive diapause ends and overwintering colonies begin to initiate their northward migration back to the U.S. But it is during the four months of winter that the colony sites are open to ecotourism, receiving upwards of a quarter-million visitors each year. Augmented by highway infrastructure between surrounding towns and an inherent desire to witness this spectacular event, a tourism culture has grown around monarchs. There are now hotels, restaurants and shops in Zitacuaro, Ocampo, and, Angangueo. Infrastructure at each colony site has also grown, with parking lots, vendors, small restaurants, guide services and horse rentals now available at public entrances. In most cases, after an hour's walk or horseback ride from an entrance station, visitors arrive at the monarch colonies where tens of millions of monarchs are roosting, flying, sipping water at small puddles, and covering the vegetation.

Since the world found out about the amazing winter habitat of the monarch, it's been a growing tourist attraction. Today, hundreds of thousands of visitors come to a relatively localized area of Mexico to behold this magical sight.

While roughly 12 permanent colony
sites are known, only four are open
to the public. These tend to be the
largest colonies year after year,
rewarding visitors with a dazzling
display of orange and black. Butterflies
cover the trees and soar through the
air in great numbers on warm days.

More than 90 percent of the visitors
to the monarch reserves are Mexican
tourists, demonstrating the great passion,
love and interest Mexican citizens have
for the natural wonders of their country.

It is critical that new generations be
exposed to the migration and the science
behind it if the migration is to remain a
healthy phenomenon for our children
and children's children to appreciate.

Through responsible tourism, visitors may get the show of a lifetime, and photos to go along with it. From puddling butterflies right on the trail to magnificent viewpoints into the heart of the colony, it is an overwhelming sensation to observe millions of butterflies all around you.

In addition to the spectacle of the butterflies, local park rangers offer interpretation and explanation of the migratory event. For international visitors, several organizations offer guided expeditions to the monarch sanctuaries where visitors can learn firsthand from community naturalists and biologists.

The monarch colonies can be a very spiritual experience for many.

A mural in the town of Angangueo
proudly displays the butterflies'
life cycle on a school wall.

From hotels to restaurants to art shops, local people are able to realize economic gain from the monarchs. Earning income from tourism is a great benefit to local communities. By linking economic incentives to the butterflies and their migration, value is added to the monarchs' natural habitat. The more valuable the forest and butterflies become, the less likely their forest habitat is to be logged or transformed into agricultural land—a common threat in many countries around the world.

A local Mexican man weaves baskets from fallen pine needles, turning them into works of art for sale near the sanctuaries.

Singers and mariachis provide local color and celebrate the monarchs' arrival each year.

A sign in Angangueo directs visitors toward the nearby El Rosario sanctuary.

Local beliefs have not always favored the monarch. For many years their arrival and departure was a mysterious omen, often linked with death and the afterlife. However, as ecotourism improves the welfare of local communities, the monarchs are embraced and welcomed as never before. The monarchs' welfare is now keenly linked to the health of the community and the environment.

SANTUARIO
EL ROSARIO
El mas grande
del Mundo
A 12 Kms.
Nuevo
TV
contigo

Enthusiasm for monarch butterflies
is unparalleled. This tiny animal has
captured the hearts and minds of
millions of people. From a conservation
perspective, the more advocates the
butterfly has, the brighter its future in the
face of environmental challenges.

Be sure to check your bag before putting it on your back! Monarchs, like most species of butterflies, take advantage of ingesting salt whenever and wherever possible.

As ecotourism grows, so too does
the support from the local ejidos,
or communities, around the
reserves. Each reserve is owned
and managed by local villagers,
creating stakeholders and
invested advocates. A new mural
emerges to greet visitors at the
entrance to one of the reserves.

PAIS DE LA MONARCA
MONARCH BUTTERFLY COUNTRY

A local truck warmly welcomes
visitors from around the world.
As international attention turns
to ecotourism, the monarch
migration phenomenon stands to
increase markedly in popularity.

FARMACIA
SIMILARES
"RoS
SIN VENTA
COBERTORES

Despite its growing international reputation, the small town of Angangueo remains humble and authentic. With roots originally in the mining industry, most local jobs now revolve around the monarch migration in some way, shape or form.

DISCOVERING OUR
PLANET
TOGETHER
natural habitat
WWF

As a guide and a scientist, each year
I take eager travelers to these overwintering butterfly
sanctuaries for photography, observation and a life-
changing encounter. The moment someone sees a
vast butterfly colony for the first time is not only a trip
highlight for them, but it is repeatedly a revelation for
me as well. Witnessing the reactions at that moment
of discovery is like a rebirth of the senses. Often
my guests have dreamed of this moment since they
first learned of the migration's existence. When it
materializes before their eyes, their faces light up with
wonder and astonishment. I am instantly transported
back to the very first time I set my eyes on the millions
of butterflies in these monarch biosphere reserves. It
sounds cliched, but it's a moment I will never forget. I
had climbed by horseback into these beautiful forests,
seeing one, two, four butterflies floating down the
forest trail. Suddenly, I looked up at what appeared
to be a blanket of orange and brown leaves dangling
off every fir bough...these were the monarchs. As I

ventured deeper into the colony, millions were swirling
in spectacular flight as yellow sunbeams broke through
the tops of the trees. Simply magical.

I am also a conservation biologist. It's difficult to say
which came first, my passion for guiding or my fervor
for saving our planet's wild places and wildlife. But one
thing is certain: these two professions and purposes
are deeply intertwined. One of my major incentives for
guiding people to these hallowed sanctuaries is to raise
awareness and create new influencers from all over the
world who want to help preserve nature.

The monarch as a species is incredibly numerous.
Given its worldwide distribution, it cannot be listed
as an endangered species—nor would I necessarily
advocate for that. However, the migratory phenomenon
is indeed endangered. There is a delicate balance
of habitat, climate and food sources that absolutely
must be intact for the migration to occur. If any single

segment of the main ingredients is out of whack, the entire event could collapse. Considering that each of these elements is among the most critical global conservation concerns, there are reasons to feel unsettled.

But monarchs are one of the most recognizable animal species on Earth, and they have a growing cadre of supporters. Throughout the past several decades, this support has translated into protection, education and advocacy. While habitat loss issues stretch across international borders, from deforestation in Mexico to agricultural conversion of their North American habitat in the U.S. and Canada, there is hope. Yearly deforestation in Mexican overwintering grounds is at a record low, and habitat conversion in the U.S. and Canada is receiving more attention than ever—both from the public and private sectors. However, it's difficult to say whether these improvements will be enough to

provide substantial food for larvae and adults during their summer breeding period. Similarly, a sudden jump in Mexico's deforestation could open up the forest and leave the butterflies vulnerable to winter storms, which are increasingly frequent and erratic due to a changing climate. Simply put, the monarch's survival depends upon interconnected, landscape-scale forces that don't change overnight.

At the end of this book, a resource page provides information about many great organizations that are working to protect the monarch butterfly in a variety of capacities. On the list are groups focused on everything from tutorials to make-your-own-backyard-monarch habitat to monarch population research to government policy work. I encourage you to explore these organizations and their inspiring work.

Ecotourism and conservation are distinctly connected. Through conservation travel, you are adding direct value to natural areas by showing local people that the field or forest is more valuable left intact. Your visit demonstrates that visitors will pay to experience the natural areas as whole ecosystems, versus chopped down or plowed over for short-term gains via timber harvesting or livestock grazing.

Local people in developing countries must put food on their tables, and this is a critical part of the conservation discussion that must remain center stage. That's why conservation travel works: We are proving that people stand to make significantly more money, putting more and better food on local tables. Conservation travel spreads the wealth throughout entire villages, towns, and cities, instead of among just a few people who might make a quick dollar from permanently altering a landscape via deforestation or hunting. The success of conservation travel for communities and species has been proven time and time again across the world. Monarch butterflies and their migration present yet another opportunity for local people to benefit greatly by protecting an exceptional natural resource.

While scenes such as this are relatively common in the sanctuaries, overall monarch numbers are on a downward trend from year to year. Scientists are concerned that large-scale pressures such as habitat loss and climate change could dramatically reduce the populations, causing a crash at some point.

Surveys from 2012-2016 have shown that illegal logging has slowed dramatically in Mexican forests—a great conservation success story in the area. Reducing deforestation has been a focus of critical attention in recent decades.

Monarchs need trees not only as places to roost, but also for the unique microclimate they create. Within dense stands of these oyamel trees, the temperature is slightly warmer, the winds are less strong and the humidity is higher—all conditions that monarchs have come to depend upon.

If logging is allowed, even plucking out single trees, the specific microclimate could be altered drastically, as if there is a hole in the blanket that holds in steady temperatures.

It's one long journey...here, a
single monarch rests during the
latter part of winter.

Monarchs are found around the world,
including Australia, South America, Europe
and even Hawaii. However, most researchers
believe they began as a neotropical species,
originating somewhere in the southern range
of North America or Central America. They
then dispersed from there to colonize the
rest of North America due to an abundance
of milkweed, their food source as caterpillars,
in the more temperate zones of the nothern
U.S. and southern Canada.

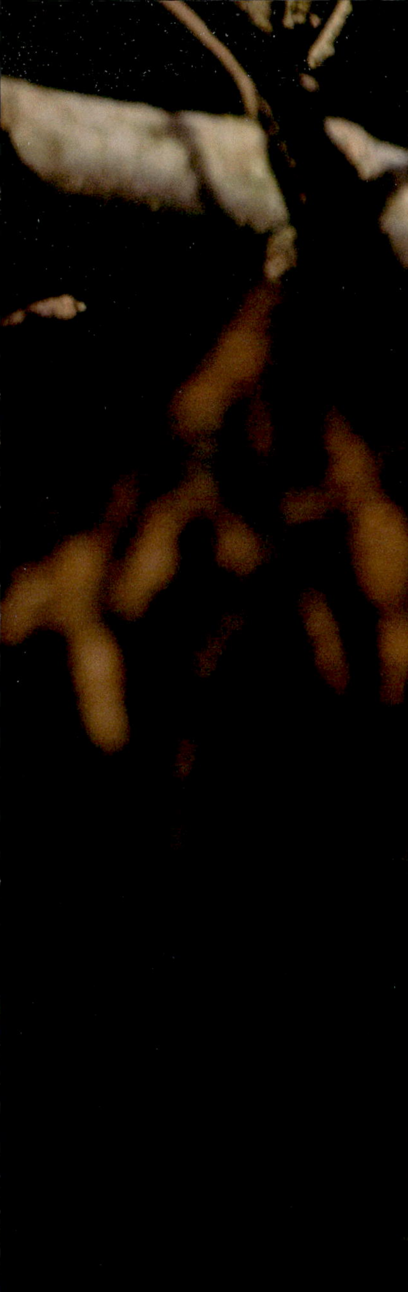

A monarch rests on a dying
fir tree—a symbolic image of
what the forests may look like if
monarch populations continue to
decline without relief.

Although large commercial logging operations
have all but vanished, smaller one-man
operations still continue to be a threat. Even
if the majority of trees are allowed to remain,
the selective logging of individual (and often
the largest) trees completely changes the
composition of the forest, jeopardizing its
overall health.

There are many reasons for hope. Conservation groups in Mexico, such as WWF and others, are actively reforesting areas in and around the biosphere reserves. Here, a small commercial nursery grows oyamel saplings to sell to reforestation programs—a novel way to incentivize conservation while directly contributing to the local economy.

A member of the local El Rosario ejido sells individual saplings at the reserve entrance.

SE VENDEN
ARBOLES $10
REGLAMENTO
TAQUILLA N°2

WWF
YVES ROCHER
FONDATION
SOUS L'ÉGIDE DE L'INSTITUT DE FRANCE

Today, there is significant multinational support for the monarch. In addition to more hands-on projects like reforestation, international NGOs actively work with the governments of Canada, the U.S. and Mexico to form agreements on policy and protection for the forests and monarchs, which call all three countries home during different parts of their life cycle.

Ecotourism is one of the key solutions for raising awareness, and funds to protect the monarch and its various habitats. It turns the former loggers into forest rangers and guides, showing local people that there is a better, more sustainable and long-term way to earn a living by protecting the surrounding forests.

TOURS A LA MONARCA

Perhaps the most incredible part of the monarch story is how much there is still to learn and discover. Despite being one of the most well-studied insects in the world, new studies of monarchs are uncovering fascinating findings year after year. Whether linking their health with the condition of a surrounding ecosystem, providing insight into their intricate navigation techniques, or uncovering more of a complex genome responsible for all they're able to accomplish, a great many people are discovering an ever greater number of insights into our world via the monarch.

It is my sincere hope that this book inspires you in many ways, including fostering a wanderlust to witness the monarch migration phenomenon in person. I encourage you to make one of the best wildlife expeditions you've ever experienced. But also, I hope it inpires you to dig deeper and learn more about our natural world. The monarch is

an ideal lens through which to interpret and understand the intricacies and complexities of interconnected life on our planet. The monarch life cycle has been taught in school classrooms for years for this very reason. In addition to being an aesthetically pleasing species, monarchs are surprisingly easy to care for, whether you are interested in breeding them, having an outside garden with milkweed as a larval food source, or creating a full-fledged monarch waystation with adult nectaring habitat along their migration route. A comprehensive resource list for learning more about all these topics is at the back of this book.

And lastly, what I feel is perhaps most important is for you to share your own wonder, curiosity and passion for the natural world with someone else. Whether it be a friend, brother, sister, son, granddaughter or even someone you meet in the gardening section of a home improvement store,

spreading the message and creating awareness is one of
the most powerful outcomes for education, ecotourism and
conservation. Together we can and will save the monarch
and its magnificent migration for many generations to come.

Ecotourism is a key solution to raising awareness and funding protection for monarchs and their various habitats. Ecotourism turns former loggers into forest rangers and guides, showing local people a better, more sustainable and long-term way to earn a living by protecting the forests.

While the monarch migration
phenomenon has been known to the
world for several decades, the feeling
of discovery is still palpable in the
enchanting forests of the Sierra Madre.
What surprises most visitors to these
sanctuaries is the forest's intrinsic beauty
and peace.

Monarchs and their Mexican forest create a metaphor for life. As we turn the corner, there is always something new to discover and marvel over.

❧ Acknowledgements ❧

Having embarked on a 17-year journey with the monarchs to date, I must thank numerous people who were pivotal to the culmination of publishing this book. In addition to many key mentors, professors and fellow naturalist guides, the terrific friends I've met along the way were integral. From researching and learning about the migratory phenomenon in the first place, to honing my photographic skills, to letting me use their department's scanning electron microscope to research the acoustic organs and antennal structure of these creatures, it took a village…

And, of course, to the two most influential people in my life, my mother, Lee, and my wife, Katie—there just simply aren't words to describe how much I've learned and benefited from your guidance, patience and love.

Here's to you all, and to the inspiring monarch butterfly.

❧ Resources ❧

Monarch Watch
www.MonarchWatch.org

Monarch Joint Venture
www.MonarchJointVenture.org

World Wildlife Fund Monarch Squad
www.worldwildlife.org/species/monarch-butterfly

Shady Oak Butterfly Farm
www.butterfliesetc.com

Journey North Monarch Tracker
www.learner.org/jnorth/monarch/

McGuire Center for Lepidoptera & Biodiversity
www.floridamuseum.ufl.edu/mcguire/

Monarch Butterfly Conservation Fund
www.nfwf.org/monarch/Pages/home.aspx

onso-Mejia, A., E. Rendon-Salinas, E. Montesinos-Patino, and L. P. Brower. 1997. se of lipid stores in Monarch butterflies overwintering in Mexico: implications for onservation. Ecological Applications 7:934–947.

arker, J. F. and W. S. Herman. 1976. Effect of photoperiod and temperature n reproduction of the Monarch butterfly (Danaus plexippus). Journal of Insect hysiology 22:1565–1568.

arkin, D. 2003. Alleviating poverty through ecotourism: promises and reality in e Monarch reserve in Mexico. Environment, Development, and Sustainability 371–382.

aur, R., M. Haribal, A. Renwick, and E. Stadler. 1998. Contact chemoreception lated to host selection and oviposition in the Monarch butterfly, Danaus plexippus. hysiological entomology 23:7–19.

ackiston, D., A. D. Briscoe, and M. R. Weiss. 2010. Color vision and learning in the onarch butterfly, Danaus plexippus (Nymphalidae). The Journal of Experimental ology 214:509–520.

oppre, M. 1993. The American Monarch: courtship and chemical communication of peculiar Danaine butterfly. Pages 29-41 in S. B. Malcolm and M. P. Zalucki, editors. ology and conservation of the Monarch butterfly. Natural History Museum of Los ngeles County, Los Angeles, California, USA.

ower, A. V. Z. N. Wahlberg, J. R. Ogawa, M. Boppre, and R. Vane-Wright. 2010. hylogenetic relationships among genera of danaine butterflies (Lepidoptera: ymphalidae) as implied by morphology and DNA sequences. Systematics and odiversity 8:75–89.

ower, L. P. 1961. Studies on the migration of the Monarch butterfly I. Breeding opulations of Danaus plexippus and Danaus gilippus berenice in south central orida. Ecology 42:76–83.

ower, L. P., W. H. Calvert, L. E. Hendrick, and J. Christian. 1977. Biological oservations on an overwintering colony of monarch butterflies (Danaus plexippus, anaidae) in Mexico. Journal of the Lepidopterists' Society 31:232–242.

ower, L. P. 1985. New perspectives on the migration biology of the Monarch utterfly, Danaus plexippus L. Pages 748–785 in M. A. Ranking, editor. Migration: echanisms and adaptive significance. University of Texas Contributions in Marine cience, Austin, Texas, USA.

ower, L. P. 1988. Avian predation on the monarch butterfly and its implications for imicry theory. The American Naturalist 131:S4–S6.

ower, L. P. 1995. Understanding and misunderstanding the migration of the onarch butterfly (Nymphalidae) in North America: 1857-1995. Journal of the epidopterists' Society 49:304–385.

own, J. J., and G. M. Chippendale. 1974. Migration of the Monarch butterfly, Danaus exippus: energy sources. Journal of Insect Physiology 20:17–30.

alvert, W. H. and L. P. Brower. 1986. The location of Monarch butterfly (Danaus exippus L.) overwintering colonies in Mexico in relation to topography and climate. ournal of the Lepidopterists' Society 40:164–187.

alvert, W. H., S. B. Malcolm, J. I. Glendinning, L. P. Brower, P. Zalucki, T. Van Hook, B. Anderson, and L. C. Snook. 1988. Conservation biology of Monarch butterfly verwintering sites in Mexico. Vida Silvestre Neotropica 2:38–48.

Crewe, T. L., J. D. McCracken, and D. Lepage. 2007. Population trend analysis of Monarch butterflies using daily counts during fall migration at Long Point, Ontario, Canada (1995-2006). United States Fish and Wildlife Service Publishing, Arlington, Virginia, USA.

de la Maza, E. J. and W. H. Calvert. 1993. Investigations of possible Monarch butterfly overwintering areas in central and southeastern Mexico. Pages 295–297 in S. B. Malcolm and M. P. Zalucki, editors. Biology and conservation of the Monarch butterfly. Publications of the Los Angeles County Museum of Natural History, Los Angeles, California, USA.

Gibbs, D. R., R. K. Walton, L. P. Brower, and A. K. Davis. 2005. Monarch butterfly (Lepidoptera: Nymphalidae) migration monitoring at Chincoteague, Virginia and Cape May, New Jersey: a comparison of long-term trends. Journal of the Kansas Entomological Society 79:156–164.

Glendinning, J. I., A. Alonso, and L. P. Brower. 1988. Behavioral and ecological interactions between foraging mice (Peromyscus melanotis) and overwintering monarch butterflies (Danaus plexippus) in Mexico. Oecologia 75:222–227.

Goehring, L. and K. S. Oberhauser. 2004. Environmental factors influencing post-diapause reproductive development in Monarch butterflies. Pages 187–195 in K. S. Oberhauser and M. Solensky, editors. The Monarch butterfly: biology and conservation. Cornell University Press, Ithaca, New York, USA.

Guerra, P. A., C. Merlin, R. J. Gegear, and S. M. Reppert. 2012. Discordant timing between antennae disrupts sun compass orientation in migratory Monarch butterflies. Nature Communications 958:1–7.

Herman, W. S. 1981. Studies on the adult reproductive diapause of the Monarch butterfly. Biological Bulletin 160:89–106.

Herman, W. S. 1986. Hormonally mediated events in adult Monarch butterflies. Pages 800–815 in M. A. Rankin, editor. Migration mechanisms and adaptive significance. University of Texas Contributions in Marine Science, Austin, Texas, USA.

Herman, W. S., L. P. Brower, and W. H. Calvert. 1989. Reproductive tract development in Monarch butterflies overwintering in California and Mexico. Journal of the Lepidopterists' Society 43:50–58.

James, D. G. 1986. Effect of temperature upon energy reserves of the Monarch butterfly, Danaus plexippus (L) (Lepidoptera, Danaidae). Australian Journal of Zoology 34:373–379.

Jones, D. S. and B. J. MacFadden. 1982. Induced magnetization in the monarch butterfly, Danaus plexippus (Insecta, Lepidoptera). Journal of Experimental Biology 96:1–9.

Malcolm, S. B. 1993. Spring recolonization of eastern North America by the Monarch butterfly: successive brood or single sweep migration? Pages 253–267 in S. B. Malcolm and M. P. Zalucki, editors. Biology and conservation of the Monarch butterfly. Natural History Museum of Los Angeles County, Los Angeles, California, USA.

Malcolm, S. B. and M. P. Zalucki. 1993. Biology and conservation of the Monarch butterfly. Natural History Museum of Los Angeles County, Los Angeles, California. USA.

Masters, A. R., S. B. Malcolm, and L. P. Brower. 1988. Monarch butterfly (Danaus plexippus) thermoregulatory behavior and adaptations for overwintering in Mexico. Ecology 69:458–467.

Meitner, C. J., L. P. Brower, and A. K. Davis. 2004. Migration patterns and environmental effects on stopover of Monarch butterflies (Lepidoptera: Nymphalidae) at Peninsula Point, Michigan. Environmental Entomology 33:249–256.

Merlin, C., R. G. Gegear, and S. M. Reppert. 2009. Antennal circadian clocks coordinate sun compass orientation in migratory monarch butterflies. Science 325:1700–1704.

Mouritsen, H. and Frost, B.J. 2002. Virtual migration in tethered flying Monarch butterflies reveals their orientation mechanisms. Proceedings of the National Academy of Sciences USA 99:10162–10166.

Oberhauser, K. S. and R. S. Hampton. 1995. The relationship between mating and oogenesis in Monarch butterflies (Lepidoptera: Danainae). Journal of Insect Behavior 8:701–713.

Oberhauser, K. S., I. Gebhard, C. Cameron, and S. Oberhauser. 2007. Parasitism of Monarch butterflies (Danaus plexippus) by Lespesia archippivora (Diptera: Tachinidae). American Midland Naturalist 157:312–328.

Reppert, S. M. 2007. The ancestral circadian clock of Monarch butterflies: role in time-compensated sun compass orientation. Quantitative Biology 72:113–118.

Reppert, S. M., H. Zhu, and R. H. White. 2004. Polarized light helps Monarch butterflies navigate. Current Biology 14:155–158.

Reppert, S. M., R. G. Gegear, and C. Merlin. 2010. Navigational mechanisms of migrating Monarch butterflies. Trends in Neurosciences 33:399–406.

Rothschild, M. and G. Bergstrom. 1997. The Monarch butterfly caterpillar (Danaus plexippus) waves at passing hymenoptera and passing jet aircraft—are repellent volatiles released simultaneously? Phyochemistry 45:1139–1144.

Urquhart, F. A. 1960. The monarch butterfly. University of Toronto Press, Toronto, Canada.

Urquhart, F. A. 1966. A study of the migrations of gulf coast populations of the Monarch butterfly (Danaus plexippus L.) in North America. Annales Zoologici Fennici 3:82–86.

Urquhart, F. A. and N. R. Urquhart. 1976. The overwintering site of the eastern population of the Monarch butterfly (Danaus p. plexippus; Danaidae). Journal of the Lepidopterists' Society 30:153–158.

Urquhart, F. A. and N. R. Urquhart. 1978. Autumnal migration routes of the eastern population of the Monarch butterfly (Danaus p. plexippus L.; Danaidae: Lepidoptera) in North America to the overwintering site in the neovolcanic plateau of Mexico. Canadian Journal of Zoology 56: 1759–64.

Walton, R. K. and L. P. Brower. 1996. Monitoring the fall migration of the Monarch butterfly Danaus plexippus L. (Nymphalidae: Danaidae) in eastern North America: 1991-1994. Journal of the Lepidopterists' Society 50:1–10.

Walton, R. K., L. P. Brower, and A. K. Davis 2005. Long-term monitoring and fall migration patterns of the Monarch butterfly in Cape May, New Jersey. Annals of the Entomological Society of America 98:682–689.

Zhu, H., R. J. Gegear, A. Casselman, S. Kanginakudru, and S. M. Reppert. 2009. Defining behavioral and molecular differences between summer and migratory Monarch butterflies. BMC Biology 7:1–14.